BRUMBACK LIBRARY

3 3045 00155 2328

P9-DBH-856

$16.78

616.8553 Moragne, Wendy
MON   Dyslexia

1/00

THE BRUMBACK LIBRARY
OF VAN WERT COUNTY
VAN WERT, OHIO

DYSLEXIA

DYSLEXIA

WENDY MORAGNE

The Millbrook Medical
Library

The Millbrook Press
Brookfield, Connecticut

6168553
MON

MAB

Library of Congress Cataloging–in–Publication Data
Moragne, Wendy.
Dyslexia / by Wendy Moragne.
p.   cm.— (The Millbrook medical library)
Includes bibliographical references and index.
Summary: Explains the nature of dyslexia, the various forms
of treatment, and the many challenges faced by those living
with this condition. Includes case studies and interviews.
ISBN 0-7613-0206-9 (lib. bdg.)
1. Dyslexia—Juvenile literature. [1. Dyslexia.] I. Title. II. Series.
RJ496.A5M66   1997
616.85'53—dc20   96-31119 CIP AC

Photographs courtesy of Monkmeyer: pp. 16 (© Jeffrey Dunn), 35 (© Steve
Goldberg), 59 (© Spencer Grant), 62 (© Rhoda Sidney), 77 (© Kathleen Marie
Menke); Science Source/Photo Researchers: pp. 24 (© Will & Deni McIntyre),
41 (© S. I. U.); Photo Edit: p. 45 (© Bonnie Kamin); The Image Works pp. 50
(© Elizabeth Crews), 71 (© W. Hill, Jr.), 79 (© Julie Stovall/From The Hip).

Published by The Millbrook Press, Inc.
Brookfield, Connecticut

Copyright ©1997 by Wendy Moragne
All rights reserved
5 4 3 2

16.78

To Renee Tursi, who believed I could write a book, and to Kate Nunn, who gave me the opportunity to do so.

CONTENTS

WHO'S WHO

In this book, you will meet nine young people who have worked hard to meet the challenges posed by dyslexia, a disorder that involves difficulty with language. You will hear them describe the struggles they have faced, especially in school, and what they are doing to overcome or cope with their problems. You will also learn what their teachers and family members are doing to help them achieve success in their endeavors. These courageous teenagers share their stories hoping that their experiences will inspire as well as teach you.

Tim, 18 years old
Tim struggled in and out of school, prompting criticism from his teachers and parents and ridicule from his classmates and teammates. As a result, Tim developed behavior problems, which eventually led his parents to seek the help of a psychologist. The psychologist diagnosed Tim with dyslexia and recommended that he be given special instruction at school. The special instruction, combined with help from his family, have helped Tim to do well

enough in school that he will soon attend college to study engineering.

David, 18 years old

David's symptoms were so severe that he was forced to repeat first grade, although he was not diagnosed with dyslexia until he reached third grade. David benefitted from receiving special instruction at school, and he is now working toward graduating from high school. He is planning a career in marine mechanics.

Gregory, 15 years old

Gregory's sense of humor has helped him cope with the problems he has faced as a result of being dyslexic. His fun-loving, outgoing nature has also won him many friends. Gregory's school performance has improved as a result of the special instruction he has received, but his greatest achievements have been in acting.

Lisa, 15 years old

The constant failure that Lisa faced as a result of being dyslexic eventually caused her to drop out of school during ninth grade. She chose, instead, to spend her days at the horse stables where she rides. Lacking self-confidence, she felt worthwhile only when she was helping with the horses. After learning that Lisa's problems stemmed from dyslexia, Lisa's parents assured her that she could be helped, and they encouraged her to return to school. She is doing better in school and works at the stables in her spare time, saving her money so that she can buy her own horse.

Kristin, 17 years old

Kristin, a senior in high school, is looking forward to becoming a professional ballerina after graduation. She feels that the hard work she has had to apply to her schoolwork parallels the hard work she has had to apply to dancing. Both have required self-discipline and determination. Kristin feels that she has been able to achieve success in school as well as in dance because of the support and encouragement she has received from her mother.

Jennifer, 16 years old
Jennifer's confusion over the sounds of letters and of words hampered her efforts at reading. She often mispronounced words and misheard what was said. As a result of her difficulties, her classmates teased her and she argued with her family. With regular help at school, Jennifer has made progress. She now has a good relationship with her sister and her parents, who help her do her schoolwork. Jennifer is also learning to accept her mistakes and to use them to learn and grow.

Amanda, 14 years old
Because her symptoms were mild, Amanda was not evaluated for reading, spelling, and writing problems until she reached high school, where an observant English teacher suspected that she was dyslexic. Amanda regularly meets with a tutor, which helps her keep up with her classmates. In addition, Amanda's teachers make certain accommodations for her, such as giving her extra time on tests and allowing her to use a word processor for written assignments. Her grades have improved.

Ryan, 13 years old
Ryan's parents picked on Ryan because of his poor grades. Although he tried his best, he struggled in all of his classes except art, in which he excelled. The disappointment that Ryan's parents expressed over their only son's failures led Ryan to feel sad and angry. He eventually distanced himself from his parents. After Ryan was diagnosed with dyslexia, his parents began to understand the nature of the disorder, were more accepting of his weaknesses, and focused on his talents in art instead.

Jeff, 16 years old
Jeff's school struggles caused him to feel inferior to his two older brothers, whose achievements were outstanding. Jeff's parents pressured him to compete with his brothers and to achieve what they had achieved, but he found it impossible to measure up to his parents' expectations. The turning point for Jeff came after he was diagnosed with dyslexia. His parents allowed him to join the wrestling team, and he became the only undefeated wrestler in his school. His success in wrestling and the progress he is making at school have helped him develop positive feelings about himself.

Chapter One

WHAT IS DYSLEXIA?

TIM'S STORY

As a young child, Tim was fun-loving and engaging. His mild manner and happy nature charmed his parents and delighted his older brother and younger sister. But when he began school, the challenges that Tim faced cast a shadow on his easygoing manner.

In kindergarten, Tim found it difficult to learn the letters of the alphabet, and he often confused left and right, and up and down. Learning to print his name was difficult for him, also. "TIM" sometimes turned out as "TIW" or "MIT" or "WIT."

In the primary grades, Tim struggled with learning to read. He sometimes confused words that looked similar, and often lost his place on the page. There were even times when he read words backward. When writing, Tim made many spelling errors, and his handwriting was scrawled in letters of different sizes. Even math, his favorite subject, often gave him trouble. He sometimes reversed numbers or confused mathematical signs, such as "+" and "x," or "-" and "=." Tim's problems forced him to work slowly and, as a result, he usually found it impossible to complete assignments on time. He eventually became the object of ridicule and rejection by classmates. Even his teachers and parents began to criticize him.

"Tim's brother and sister were such good students," says Tim's mother. "We couldn't understand why Tim was having so much trouble. We thought that he wasn't applying himself. Even his teachers felt that his problems were the result of laziness. We began to nag him to improve."

Tim experienced problems outside of school, too. He enjoyed riding his bicycle, but often found it difficult to find his way home, even when he was in his own neighborhood. He arrived home late so many times that his parents finally took away his bicycle as punishment. When he joined the community softball team, he had more trouble.

"I was an okay hitter," Tim recalls, "but many times—too many times—after I hit the ball, I ran toward third base instead of first base. I got confused because of my problem with direction. My teammates were totally unforgiving. They called me all sorts of names, and I ended up in fist fights, which eventually got me thrown off the team.

"My life was a mess. No matter how hard I tried to make things work out, I never could. My teachers were always impatient with me, and I knew my parents were disappointed in me. I didn't have any friends because other kids thought I was a real dope. I couldn't please anyone. I hated the way I was, but I couldn't help it."

By the time Tim reached middle school, his problems had gotten the better of him. His once mild manner dissolved into hostile defiance. He began to rebel against almost anything his parents asked of him, and he picked fights with his brother and sister.

"I felt so angry inside," says Tim. "My parents praised my brother and sister for everything they did and criticized me for everything I did. I felt bad about not being able to measure up to what they wanted me to be, but I resented that they never gave me the benefit of the doubt. They never gave me credit for trying my best. I got to the point where I wanted to be mean and nasty around them to get even for the way they were treating me. And I felt angry and resentful toward Paul and Heather because I envied their success and the good treatment they got from my parents."

"Our family needed help," says Tim's mother. "Tim's problems at school were bad enough, but when Tim became belligerent at home, things became unbearable for us as a family. That's when we decided to take him to a psychologist. She diagnosed him with dyslexia and recommended that he be given special instruction at school to help him strengthen his skills. She also recommended ways for our family to help Tim achieve success both in and out of school."

Today, Tim is eighteen years old and is completing his senior year of high school. The special instruction he has received at school has helped him make a marked improvement in his school performance. In addition, Tim's teachers have made allowances with schoolwork assignments, homework assignments, and tests, and they have let Tim do much of his written work orally or on a word processor.

Just as Tim did, many dyslexics benefit greatly from individualized instruction at school. And with the support and encouragement of family members, the chances are even greater that many of the challenges dyslexics face can be overcome.

Tim has had to work hard to achieve success, and his family has been behind him all of the way. His parents, brother, and sister have faithfully taken turns reading textbook material out loud to him and helping him with homework assignments and with studying for tests. Tim's hard work and the support of his family have paid off because Tim has been accepted to college to study engineering.

"I hope to design planes and rockets someday," says Tim. "Right now, I build remote-controlled model airplanes for a hobby, but in the future I hope to be involved in the real thing."

"Tim's mother and I feel very proud of Tim's accomplishments," says Tim's father. "It hasn't been easy for him. We're anticipating his graduation from high school with great joy, and we have high hopes for his success as a college student. Tim understands that earning his degree in engineering will be tough. He knows that he will have to work harder than most students, but he has strong determination."

UNDERSTANDING DYSLEXIA

The word "dyslexia" is derived from the Greek words *dys,* which refers to a difficulty, and *lexia,* which refers to the use of words. The condition called dyslexia refers to a difficulty using words or language, and people with this condition are called dyslexics. Dyslexics have difficulty with phonological awareness, or the ability to appreciate that spoken language is made up of individually distinct sound units. This difficulty is the core of dyslexia.

Dyslexia is not an illness or a disease. It is a brain-based disorder that causes problems for people in using oral or written language. These problems may occur in reading, writing, spelling, math, speaking, and/or listening.

DYSLEXIA IS A BRAIN-BASED DISORDER THAT CAUSES PROBLEMS FOR PEOPLE WHEN READING, WRITING, SPELLING, DOING MATH COMPUTATION, SPEAKING, AND EVEN LISTENING. DYSLEXIA IS NOT AN ILLNESS OR A DISEASE.

For example, some dyslexics scramble the order of letters in words when reading and writing, or they transpose numbers when doing math computation. Others mispronounce words or mistake what is said to them. Dyslexia is not a physical eye or ear problem, however, because the eye sees symbols normally and the ear hears sounds normally. The language-usage skills of dyslexics are not as good as they should be for people of their age or intelligence. These difficulties do not result from a lag in their development, but rather from differences in the structure and function of the dyslexic's brain.

Dyslexia is considered a learning disability. Young people with the disorder often are mistakenly thought of as stupid, lazy, or rebellious. The truth is that dyslexics usually are bright and creative. Most have average or above average intelligence. Unfortunately, the problems these young people have in using language tend to get in the way of their school progress.

Who Is Dyslexic?

Tim's story may help you to better understand the nature of dyslexia and what it is like to be dyslexic, but no two people experience dyslexia in exactly the same way.

An estimated 15 percent of all people are dyslexic, which means that dyslexia affects millions of people, regardless of race, age, or gender. Dyslexia is inherited, so a dyslexic is likely to have a parent, grandparent, cousin, brother, or sister who is also dyslexic.

What Are the Symptoms of Dyslexia?

People who are classified as dyslexic have a lack of awareness of phonemes in written or spoken language.
Phonemes are the smallest sound units of language. The
"b" in "bat" is a phoneme, for example. Because they
lack phonological awareness, dyslexics tend to have trouble connecting letters with their correct sounds, distinguishing whether sounds are the same or different, sepa-
rating words into their parts, and blending parts of words
together.

Some dyslexics add or omit words when reading or
writing. Others confuse the letters in words, reading or
writing "buck" or "puck" instead of "duck," for example.
Still others sometimes read or write words backward, such
as "saw" instead of "was" or "tub" instead of "but."
Most dyslexics have trouble with spelling and have poor
handwriting. Many also have difficulty with math. They
may transpose numbers; instead of adding "32" and "58,"
they may add "23" and "85," for example.

Because reading, writing, spelling, and math are basic
learning skills, dyslexic students are at a disadvantage in
school. They tend to fall behind their classmates in their
school performance, which often causes them to feel frustrated and angry. Although most of these students are
actually trying very hard to succeed, it is common for them
to be criticized for being lazy or rebellious. This just adds
to the hardships they already face.

**DYSLEXIA AFFECTS MILLIONS OF PEOPLE, RE-
GARDLESS OF RACE, AGE, INCOME, OR GENDER.**

In addition to problems in school subjects, many
dyslexics have problems in other areas. For example, some
mispronounce words when they speak or mishear what is

said to them. Others confuse left and right or become lost when trying to get from place to place.

Before a correct diagnosis is made, the problems these young people face often cause them to fail to accomplish what is expected of them. As a result, it is common for them to experience a great deal of embarrassment and frustration both in and out of school. Fortunately, however, once a diagnosis is made and more is understood about dyslexia, most of them can get the help they need. With help, most are capable of breaking the pattern of failure and achieving success.

TYPES OF TREATMENT

Unfortunately, there is no cure for dyslexia. It is a life-long condition. The good news, however, is that most dyslexics can learn to overcome their problems through special instruction. Dyslexics are helped most when they receive direct instruction in phonics; when the instruction is designed to meet their individual needs; when the instruction involves their senses of seeing, hearing, speaking, and touching; and when it is systematic and sequential (when it progresses from simple to more complex in terms of letter-sound relationships and phonics rules). This type of instruction is called "multisensory structured language instruction."

Chapter Two discusses the symptoms of dyslexia in more detail and may help you to recognize some of these symptoms in yourself or in someone you know.

SIGNS AND SYMPTOMS

People with dyslexia have strengths and weaknesses, just like everyone else. Some have artistic ability; some have musical talent; some have athletic ability. What sets people with dyslexia apart from other people, however, is that they all have difficulty with language. What sets dyslexics apart from each other is that no two individuals experience the disorder in exactly the same way, nor do they all show the same degree of severity of symptoms.

If you have ever typed, either on a typewriter or on a word processor, you probably have made typographical errors, or errors that come from pushing the wrong keys with your fingers. Suppose, however, that these mistakes were not something you could control with your fingers. Suppose they were mistakes that were governed by your brain. This is the type of frustration that dyslexics face.

To get an idea of what it might be like to be dyslexic, try typing quickly without looking at the keys. "Your line of pirnt maight end up liiking like this. Or it might looick lik thiz insteb off the way it shoud looick. Or it wite look lik dis. Or ti evin mit luck lite tiz." These examples illustrate what it is like for many dyslexics when they try to write.

Now try to read aloud the lines of print in quotation marks. Did you have trouble making sense out of what you read? Suppose you were criticized or teased for having trouble reading these sentences. How would you feel? Imagine having trouble every time you tried to read something. Would you feel frustrated or discouraged? Now you may have a better understanding of what it is like to be dyslexic.

The symptoms of dyslexia may be mild, moderate, or severe. Individuals who experience mild symptoms tend to be easier to help. Those with severe symptoms tend to be the most difficult to help.

CHARACTERISTIC SYMPTOMS OF DYSLEXIA

Health professionals and educators consider the types of diffculties listed below to be symptoms of dyslexia. Confusing letters or words when reading or writing, or finding it difficult to copy from the board, may not necessarily be the result of dyslexia, however. Vision problems, such as nearsightedness or farsightedness, can sometimes create symptoms similar to those of dyslexia, so it is necessary for anyone who is having trouble with reading and writing to have a complete eye examination by an eye doctor.

Likewise, hearing problems can cause people to mispronounce words or mishear what others say, so it is important for people with these problems to have their hearing tested by a health professional before assuming they are dyslexic.

Confusing and Transposing Letters, Words, and Numbers

Because of the phonological problems that characterize the disorder, people with dyslexia sometimes, but not always, confuse or transpose letters, words, and numbers. When reading or writing, they might mistake "buck" for "duck" or "form" for "from," for example. When doing math computation, they might mistake "23" for "32." Dyslexics also sometimes read or write letters upside down, which causes them to mistake certain words for other similar words, such as "wet" for "met." In math, they might mistake "6" for "9."

As a result of confusing or transposing letters, words, and numbers, dyslexics tend to have trouble making sense out of what they are reading or writing. They often will have to go back over it several times to figure out what is wrong. In math computation, their answers are often incorrect.

Problems with Spelling

Because of the trouble they have connecting letters with sounds and distinguishing the separate sounds in words, most dyslexics are poor spellers. They tend to constantly erase, cross out, and write over misspellings. These are some typical types of spelling errors:

- *Confusing letters that look or sound similar.* Certain letters that look or sound similar often confuse dyslexics. For example, many confuse "b," "d," and "p," which are similar in form and similar in sound. This confusion often causes them to misspell words, writing "dack" or "pack" instead of "back," for example.

- *Writing letters out of sequence.* Dyslexics are likely to write letters out of the correct order. "Burn" becomes "brun," "fan" becomes "fna," and "girl" becomes "gril," for example. When trying to spell words with silent letters, they sometimes transpose the silent letter, spelling "answer" as "anwser," for example. Or they might simply omit the silent letter and write "answer" as "anser."

Copying a written sentence can present a problem for a person with dyslexia. This young student has reversed letters in three words even though they are correctly spelled at the top of the page.

- *Omitting syllables.* Because of their lack of phonological awareness, dyslexics often leave out sounds in words when they spell. "Banana" might be spelled "bana," for example, or "management" might be spelled "majmint."

- *Adding syllables.* Just as they often omit syllables in words, dyslexics often add syllables. They might spell "goose" as "goois," for example, or "lizard" as "lizzared."

Problems with Handwriting and Copying

Dyslexics commonly have handwriting that is cramped or scrawled. They also tend to erase frequently. Their letters are likely to be different sizes and are likely to be reversed or written over. When writing letters that confuse them, they often write capital rather than lowercase letters because it is often easier for them to remember which way capital letters face. They may write "baby" as "BaBy" or "antidote" as "antiDote," for instance. Many also mix cursive and manuscript styles in their handwriting.

"Tim's handwriting looked like those ransom notes you see on television or in the movies," says Tim's father. "Some of the letters were capitals and some weren't. And the letters were all different sizes. His handwriting was definitely unusual."

When trying to copy written material, such as from the chalkboard, dyslexics typically lose their place, erase frequently, misspell words, leave out capitalization and punctuation, reverse letters or words, and work very slowly.

Problems with Sequencing

Some dyslexics have difficulty understanding the sequence of things and events. They often have trouble with the sequence of letters in words as well as with learning a series, such as the order of the letters of the alphabet, days of the week, or months of the year.

> **A**LTHOUGH ALL PEOPLE WITH DYSLEXIA HAVE
> DIFFICULTY WITH LANGUAGE, NO TWO INDIVID-
> UALS EXPERIENCE THE DISORDER IN EXACTLY THE
> SAME WAY—NOR DO THEY ALL HAVE THE SAME
> DEGREE OF SEVERITY OF SYMPTOMS.

Even the progression of time on a clock or the sequence of events in time can be a problem for some people
with dyslexia. They may not be able to tell the events of a
story in the order in which they happened, for example, or
they may not be able to tell about events in their own lives
in the correct order.

Problems with Orientation

Some dyslexics have problems with space and time. As a
result, it is not uncommon for them to get lost when going
from place to place or to arrive late. For them, getting
around in their own neighborhood can be as difficult as
getting around in an entirely strange place.

"My family has lived in the same neighborhood all my
life," says David. "I always had to walk to school with my
sister or with the kids next door because I couldn't find my
way there by myself. One time when my sister was sick
and our neighbors were on vacation, I had to walk alone.
I never arrived at school, and the principal called my mom.
My mom was hysterical, and she called the police and all.
They found me wandering around about a block from
school. Even though I was really close to school, I couldn't
find my way there."

Problems with Direction

Some dyslexics confuse direction, such as left and right or
up and down. Those who have this problem often find it
difficult to play certain sports, such as those involving
passing a ball to the right and to the left, for example.

Tim ran to third base instead of first base when playing softball.

Problems with Organization

Many people with dyslexia have trouble organizing themselves and their belongings. They tend to have difficulty getting to school on time and often forget the books and notebooks they need.

"I usually look a mess," laughs Gregory. "My shoes are always untied, and my shirts are buttoned wrong half the time. I used to always forget my school stuff in the morning, and I'd have to call my mom to bring it to school for me."

Difficulty Following Instructions

Following instructions, especially those with several steps, causes problems for many young people with dyslexia. As a result, they often fail to complete school assignments and household chores.

"My schoolwork was never finished," says Lisa. "I couldn't remember what I was supposed to do. At home, I had the same problem. I was always in trouble for not doing what I was supposed to do. My mom and dad both work, and there were so many times that my mom would tell me to take the dinner out of the refrigerator after school and put it in the oven at a certain temperature for a certain amount of time. I would either forget about it altogether or forget part of it. Like, I'd put the food in the oven but forget to turn the oven on. The dinner would still be raw when my parents got home. They would be furious with me, and they would say I was irresponsible."

Confusion Determining Similarities and Dissimilarities

Because of their lack of phonological awareness, when some dyslexics hear or speak words, they have difficulty distinguishing whether certain words are the same or different. The result is that they have a hard time making sense out of what they hear and read. Many times, dyslexics are confused by sounds that have the same place of articulation (the placement of the tongue or lips when a word is spoken). If they were to hear the words "time" and "dime," for example, they might believe that the two words are the same. Likewise, they might believe that "fat" and "vat" are the same, or "bin" and "pin."

- *Confusion of vowel sounds.* Some people with dyslexia have trouble distinguishing the differences in vowel sounds. They specifically often have trouble distinguishing between long and short vowel sounds. They may not distinguish the difference between "cap" and "cape" or between "men" and "mean," for example. They also are likely to confuse short vowel sounds with other short vowel sounds that sound similar, such as those in the words "not" and "net" or in the words "pit," "pat," and "pet."

- *Confusion of consonant sounds.* Just as they have difficulty distinguishing the differences in vowel sounds, some dyslexics have difficulty distinguishing the differences in consonant sounds, such as "b" and "d." They also may have trouble with consonant blends, such as "cl" or "gr." It is not uncommon for them to write blends in a transposed order, such as "caly" for "clay" or "garb" for "grab," or to leave out one of the letters of a blend, such as writing "gab" for "grab," for example.

- *Difficulty with rhyming.* Rhyming is difficult for some people with dyslexia. If they are asked to name words that rhyme with "bat," for example, they may respond with words that begin with a "b," but that do not rhyme with the word—for example, "bet," "bug," "bin," or "boat." They might even choose words that are not words at all, such as "bot."

SOME DYSLEXICS CONFUSE OR TRANSPOSE LETTERS AND NUMBERS. OTHERS CONFUSE SPATIAL DIRECTIONS OR MISPRONOUNCE WORDS. MOST ARE POOR SPELLERS AND HAVE POOR HANDWRITING.

Problems with Pronunciation

Some dyslexics scramble the pronunciation of words. For example, they may pronounce the word "animal" as "aminal" or the word "spaghetti" as "pasgetti." Others have trouble with the correct pronunciation of certain consonants and might say "felelow" for the word "fellow," for instance.

"A couple of years ago in biology class, we were talking about the digestive system," recalls Kristin. "The teacher asked for someone to explain about it, and I raised my hand. When I got to the part about saliva, I pronounced it 'salaba,' and everybody in the class started snickering and whispering. I didn't even know what I had said wrong until I got home and asked my mom."

Mishearing Words

Mishearing words creates constant problems for some people with dyslexia. A teacher might be talking about "signals," for example, which the student may hear as "sea gulls." Or the lesson might be about "toxins," which the student may hear as "taxes."

"There have been so many times that I've heard things wrong," says Kristin. "My mom teaches Sunday school, and one time someone called from our church, which is named St. Pius Church. I thought the woman said, 'Will you buy a shirt?' and I hung up on her because I thought it was one of those solicitation calls. I was so embarrassed later."

Difficulty with Oral and Written Expression

Some dyslexics have trouble finding the right words when they speak or write. Some may grasp for words when conversing with others, such as saying, "Please hand me the . . . you know . . . the things that you cut with" when asking for scissors. Others have trouble writing their thoughts.

SEVERITY OF SYMPTOMS

The degree of severity of the symptoms that people with dyslexia experience can be mild, moderate, or severe. The following outlines the characteristics of each level.

Mild Dyslexia

Young people who are mildly dyslexic tend to:
1. make errors in spelling, punctuation, and capitalization
2. make grammatical errors
3. make errors in reading comprehension
4. make errors in math

Moderate Dyslexia

Young people who are moderately dyslexic tend to:
1. make continual errors in spelling, punctuation, and capitalization
2. have difficulty with reading comprehension
3. have difficulty with math
4. need extra time to finish schoolwork and homework assignments

Severe Dyslexia

Young people who are severely dyslexic tend to:
1. spell extremely poorly
2. struggle when trying to read
3. have great difficulty with math
4. require much extra time and continual guidance and tutoring to learn new material, to finish schoolwork or homework assignments, and to prepare for tests

Students with mild or moderate dyslexia tend to earn average or below average grades in school, but with hard work and self-discipline, it is often possible for them to earn good grades.

Students with severe dyslexia tend to be unable to work independently, to do handwritten reports and term papers, or to produce large quantities of work. They typically experience so much failure that they often go through school believing that they are unintelligent.

The next chapter will focus on the ways that dyslexics can cope with their various difficulties and learn to succeed at what they do.

Chapter Three

TREATMENT OPTIONS

JENNIFER'S STORY

Jennifer's parents were so taken with their five-year-old daughter that they hardly noticed that she often mispronounced words and misheard what was said to her. When it came time for Jennifer to learn to read, she had trouble matching the sounds of letters with printed letters and the sounds of words with printed words. She confused whether letters and words were the same or different.

"Jennifer was so young," says her mother. "We assumed that in time and with practice, she would develop her reading skills. We saw no need for concern."

As time passed, however, Jennifer made little progress in reading. "I was humiliated many times in school," she says. "I can remember one time when I had to read out loud and the sentence was, 'The girl made a bird out of clay and put a fish in *its bill.' Instead I read, 'The girl mad a bed out of clay and pet a frog in its dill.' Everyone in the class burst out laughing. The teacher didn't even tell them to stop because she was laughing, too.*"

In addition to her problem with reading, Jennifer found spelling and writing very difficult. She felt unsure of the spelling of most words and, as a result, she tended to constantly erase, cross out, and write over her mistakes when doing written work. Her report card grades were poor.

"My husband and I were upset," recalls Jennifer's mother. "We felt certain that Jennifer was intelligent, yet we had to admit that her school performance did not reflect this."

Because Jennifer often misheard what was said to her, it was common for her to mistake one topic of discussion for another. If the conversation happened to be about "setting the table," for instance, Jennifer might have mistakenly heard "seeing the tape." Her mistakes caused her to become defensive and argumentative.

"The arguing became unbearable," says Jennifer's sister, Melissa, who is one year older than Jennifer. "There were so many times that Jennifer would hear one thing when my parents or I had really said another thing. Then she would insist that she was right and we were wrong. Or she would accuse us of deliberately changing the subject just to trick her. She was always crying and talking back to my parents. I got to the point where I tried to avoid being home when she was home."

"Melissa always called me names and told me that she hated me for the way I acted," says Jennifer. "She really hurt my feelings. I looked up to her and I wanted to have a close relationship with her, but I knew she didn't like being around me."

Jennifer's difficulty with understanding what

she heard also often made it hard for her to follow instructions, which caused trouble for her both at school and at home. She found it difficult to complete school assignments and household chores.

"My teachers and parents were always accusing me of not trying hard enough and of being lazy," says Jennifer. "I would get confused about what work the teacher wanted us to complete in class and for homework, but I couldn't ask her to repeat the instructions just for me. I didn't want the other kids to think I was even more stupid than they already thought I was. At home, my parents would get angry and impatient when I wouldn't do what I was supposed to do. Everyone thought I was acting this way on purpose, but the truth was that I was really trying to do things right."

Jennifer's parents eventually decided to consult with the family doctor about Jennifer's problems. After examining Jennifer and finding no apparent health problems, the doctor wanted further testing to be done. Because of Jennifer's problem with mishearing what others said, the doctor recommended that her hearing be tested to determine whether she suffered from a hearing loss, and recommended that her vision be tested because of her difficulty with reading and writing.

The hearing test was performed at a medical center where special equipment was available. The results showed no problem with Jennifer's hearing. Jennifer then saw an optometrist, or eye specialist, who used special equipment to test her eyes. He found no problem with Jennifer's vision. After reviewing the results of the hearing and vision tests, the family doctor then referred Jennifer to a psychologist, who did an evaluation to try to determine the root of Jennifer's problems.

When possible medical problems have been ruled out, often a visit to a psychologist can help determine the roots of a problem, as Jennifer's family discovered. Jennifer was tested by her psychologist and finally diagnosed as having dyslexia.

Jennifer and her parents met with Dr. Harding, the psychologist, who first spoke with Jennifer's parents and asked them questions about their family history and about Jennifer's day-to-day behavior. He wanted to gather as much information about Jennifer as possible. Jennifer's parents explained to Dr. Harding about their daughter's struggle in school and about her problems at home with the family.

Dr. Harding then met alone with Jennifer. He gave her several tests, each of which measured something specific in her abilities. These tests included:

1. *a general intelligence test, which measured Jennifer's thinking abilities*
2. *a language test, which determined how well she understood language, including her phonological awareness and written expression*
3. *a reading test, which determined the level of her reading ability as well as the type of mistakes she made*
4. *a spelling test, which determined her spelling age*
5. *a math test, which measured her ability to do computation, word problems, and money measurement*
6. *a sequencing test, which determined whether she had difficulty placing things in the right order*
7. *a test for directional confusion, which determined whether she confused left and right or up and down*
8. *a preferred hand and eye test, which determined her preferred hand and eye*
9. *a test of sense of self, which determined how she felt about herself in her day-to-day life.*

Before making a diagnosis, Dr. Harding phoned

Jennifer's teacher and discussed Jennifer's school performance with her. Dr. Harding combined the specific information about Jennifer's problems at school with her test results. He concluded that Jennifer was dyslexic and recommended that she be given special instruction to help her overcome her problems.

Jennifer began to receive special tutoring at school. At home, her parents and sister helped by taping her textbook material so that she could listen to it as many times as she needed to. In addition, Jennifer's parents and teachers wrote simple instructions for household chores and school assignments on index cards so that Jennifer would know exactly what she needed to accomplish. She could refer to the cards as many times as necessary to refresh her memory.

Today, Jennifer is a junior in high school. Her school performance has improved enough that she has even made the honor roll. Life at home is also better.

"The help I've gotten has made a big difference in my school performance," says Jennifer. "But the best thing that has happened since the diagnosis is that my sister and I have a close relationship now."

Melissa says, "Once I understood why Jennifer had acted the way she had, I felt bad about all of the names I had called her and the way I had treated her. "I've tried to make up for it by helping her as much as I can. We have a really good relationship now, and we have a lot of fun together."

THE EVALUATION

If, after the age of six and a half, a student is not progressing as he or she should be in the skills of reading and writing, the student should be tested for dyslexia. Certain tests, administered by a team of experienced professionals, are used in making a diagnosis, as they were for Jennifer. The way in which Jennifer was evaluated is typical of the way in which most students are evaluated to determine whether or not they are dyslexic. Although in Jennifer's case the testing was done by professionals in private practice, an evaluation can also be conducted by school personnel.

Whether the evaluation is done privately or through the school, it takes a team of qualified, experienced professionals to make an accurate and thorough evaluation. This team may include a medical doctor, a psychologist, a speech and language pathologist, and the classroom teacher, for example. When all the test results are taken into account, the team determines whether the student is dyslexic or whether there are other factors, such as low intelligence or physical illness, that may be interfering with the student's progress at school. The team can also determine the severity of the dyslexia symptoms.

Before a student is evaluated, a parent, teacher, or doctor should describe the evaluation process to him or her. If the student understands the tests being given, he or she is less likely to feel anxious about them beforehand or nervous while taking them.

COPING WITH THE DIAGNOSIS

Young people and their parents react in various ways to a diagnosis of dyslexia. Some young people feel worried. Others may mistakenly fear that they have an incurable disease. Some feel angry and ask, "Why me?" Parents sometimes feel guilty, assuming that they have done something wrong in the upbringing of their child to make him or her dyslexic. Others feel confused. They wonder what having dyslexia really means and what effect it will have on the future of their child and their family.

THERE IS NO CURE FOR DYSLEXIA, AND IT IS A LIFE-LONG CONDITION. BUT MOST PEOPLE WITH DYSLEXIA CAN LEARN TO OVERCOME OR COMPENSATE FOR THEIR PROBLEMS.

Once a diagnosis has been made and the nature of the condition has been explained to them, young people and their parents usually feel relieved. They are happy to finally understand what has been wrong, and they are hopeful because help is available.

"We were so relieved when the diagnosis was made," says Jennifer's mother. "There was finally an explanation for why Jennifer had struggled in school and why her behavior at home had become so argumentative and tough for us to handle. It became so much easier for us to be patient with her once we found out that she was dyslexic and we learned more about dyslexia."

Detection and help are essential to the well-being of young people with dyslexia. If the disorder is not identified and treated, dyslexic students will continue to struggle in school, and many will fail. Failure also negatively affects the self-esteem of these young people, who often end up feeling that they are stupid or worthless. The longer a student has experienced failure, the harder it is for that student to be helped.

Typically, the more severe a young person's dyslexic symptoms, the more likely it is that parents and teachers will notice the problem, and the more likely it is that the person will get help. The problems of a young person whose condition is less severe, on the other hand, may go unnoticed for a long time, and he or she may struggle without help. An increased understanding of the nature of dyslexia by young people, teachers, and parents improves the chances that even dyslexics with mild symptoms will get the special assistance they need.

REMEDIATION

There is no cure for dyslexia, but dyslexics can be helped to overcome many of their problems through remediation (the process of correcting problems). The extent to which remediation can take place and the length of time needed for success depend on the following factors.

Type of Instruction

The most important factor in helping dyslexics to overcome their problems is the type of instruction they receive, and multisensory structured language instruction is the most effective. The key elements of this type of instruction are that students are given direct instruction in phonics and that the instruction they receive is individualized, multisensory, systematic, and sequential. These key elements are detailed below.

- *Direct instruction in phonics.* Students must be taught phonological awareness, or that spoken language is made up of individually distinct sound units. They must learn that the letters of the alphabet correspond to sounds and that words are made up of these letters and sounds.

    Furthermore, students must be taught that the sounds of the letters can be blended together to make words (this is called synthetic phonics) and that words can be divided into the sounds they are made up of (this is called analytic phonics).

- *Individualized instruction.* Every student must be taught according to his or her specific needs by teachers or tutors who are trained and experienced in working to overcome the problems presented by dyslexia.

- *Multisensory instruction.* Dyslexics tend to be most successful at learning when several pathways to the brain are used simultaneously. This means that they

Using more than one of the senses while learning is one way in which dyslexics can become more familiar and comfortable with words, both written and spoken. Here a teacher works with a young child, using visual aids as he writes.

are most successful when their senses of seeing, hearing, speaking, and touching are all used at the same time during the learning process. They learn how letters and words look, how they sound, how the mouth and tongue feel when saying them, and how the hand and fingers feel when writing them.

One way for the teacher to accomplish this is to work with pictures of familiar objects and movable plastic letters to teach the student the letter-sound relationships and the formation of words. For example, the teacher holds up a picture of an object (a hat). The student uses the plastic letters to form the word for the object ("h," "a," "t"). Then the student says the word aloud, and, finally, writes the word on paper or on the chalkboard.

• *Systematic and sequential instruction.* The rules governing language must be taught in a logical, organized fashion. The instruction must also be sequential; that is, students must learn one step at a time, working in order from very simple to more complex material, always building on what they have already learned. The material progresses from simple to more complex in terms of letter-sound relationships and phonics rules.

For example, students first learn how individual letters look and what sounds correspond with these letters. Then they learn how to blend letters and sounds into words and how to break whole words into parts. Finally, they learn how to string the words together into phrases and sentences.

Frequency and Duration of Instruction

The success rate of students is affected by the number of times each week that they receive special instruction and the length of each session. The more often students receive special instruction, the more quickly they tend to learn to overcome their problems.

Individual Instruction Versus Group Instruction

Dyslexics seem to learn most successfully and most quickly when they are taught in a one-to-one setting with the instructor. This means that during a lesson, the teacher works with only one student. A one-to-one setting tends to be better than a group setting because the instructor can focus on the student's particular needs and can give him or her individual attention. The student also avoids being distracted by other students and can concentrate more easily.

The training, experience, and understanding of the person working with the student affect how much and how quickly the student can be helped to overcome his or her difficulties. The instructor may be a special educator, the classroom teacher, or a tutor.

Motivation of the Student

The most successful students tend to be those who are willing to work hard. Students are most likely to feel motivated to work hard if the material they are using for reading and writing is interesting to them.

Age of the Student

Typically, the younger the student is when he or she begins to get help, the more successful the treatment process will be and the more quickly remediation will take place. Students who are diagnosed during elementary school, for example, tend to be helped more easily and more quickly than older students. Much of the reason for this difference in the success rate seems to be that older students have suffered so much failure and criticism over the years that they no longer believe that they can be successful and no longer feel motivated to try.

OTHER STRATEGIES FOR SUCCESS

Many young people with dyslexia have found that, in addition to special instruction, the following strategies have helped them cope with the challenges presented by their condition.

Helpers

Dyslexics often have trouble organizing themselves and their belongings and usually welcome help from another person.

"Before we go to bed at night, my brother helps me pack my backpack for the next day," says Gregory. "Even though he's three years younger than I am, he's a big help. He doesn't have problems like I have. When he helps me with my stuff, I don't end up going off to school without my books and homework and then having to call my mom."

A TEAM OF QUALIFIED, EXPERIENCED PROFESSIONALS—PERHAPS INCLUDING A MEDICAL DOCTOR, PSYCHOLOGIST, SPEECH AND LANGUAGE PATHOLOGIST, AND A CLASSROOM TEACHER—CAN CONDUCT A SERIES OF TESTS TO DETERMINE WHETHER OR NOT A PERSON IS DYSLEXIC.

Many young people with dyslexia also tend to have trouble being on time, remembering to take books and homework to and from school, completing school and homework assignments, and following through on household chores. They can greatly benefit from someone else's guidance in accomplishing these tasks. Help from a brother, sister, or friend often makes the difference between success and failure. For instance, because Gregory's brother helps him pack his backpack, Gregory is sure to have everything that he needs for the next school day. This makes it more likely that he will turn in his homework and other assignments on time.

Calendars, Lists, Instruction Cards, and Recordings

Calendars are helpful tools for keeping track of important dates, such as appointments, parents' or friends' birthdays,

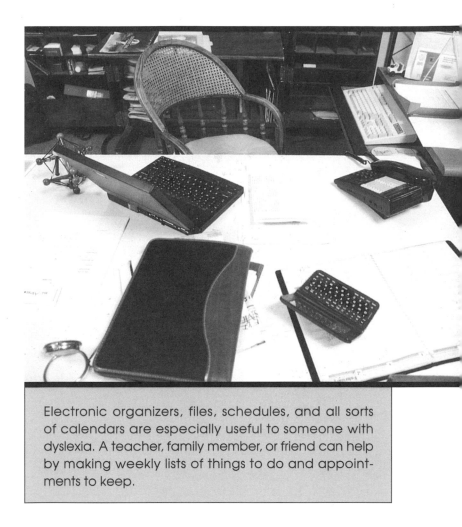

Electronic organizers, files, schedules, and all sorts of calendars are especially useful to someone with dyslexia. A teacher, family member, or friend can help by making weekly lists of things to do and appointments to keep.

upcoming parties, sports games, or performances. Due dates for school projects and reports can also be listed.

Many young people with dyslexia find it helpful when parents and teachers make daily lists of what tasks or chores they are expected to complete. Lists of household chores or school assignments help young people to keep track of what they need to do and make it easier for them to successfully complete projects.

A math teacher, for example, might make a list like this for a student:

1. In class, complete problems 1, 3, 5, 7, 9, and 11 on page 264.
2. For homework, complete problems 2, 4, 6, 8, 10 and 12 on page 265.
3. Study for a test on Friday.

Parents and teachers can also make it easier for young people who have difficulty following verbal instructions by writing simple instructions on an index card. All the steps involved in a chore or homework assignment should be listed. An instruction card written by a parent might look like this:

1. Put kitchen trash into garbage bag.
2. Put bathroom trash into garbage bag.
3. Tie top of garbage bag.
4. Carry garbage bag outside.

Instruction cards, like lists, make it easier for these young people to successfully complete what is expected of them.

Some students prefer to have instructions recorded on a tape recorder rather than written down. "My mom bought a small tape recorder that we could keep in the drawer in the kitchen," says Gregory. "Every day, she records what she wants me to do after school that day. I always get something to eat when I get home, and I listen to the tape while I'm eating. If later on I forget what I'm supposed to do, I just listen to the tape again."

The next chapter discusses the challenges that dyslexic students face in school and what can be done in the classroom and at home to make completing schoolwork and homework assignments easier for them.

Chapter Four

MEETING CHALLENGES AT SCHOOL

Learning and succeeding in school are not only challenging, but are often overwhelming goals for students with dyslexia. Despite their hard work, most of them lag behind their classmates. Some even have to repeat a grade in school. Some students with mild dyslexia symptoms miss being diagnosed. Although they have trouble at school, parents and teachers may overlook their problems or attribute them to some other cause. Students with moderate or severe symptoms are more likely to be diagnosed and helped.

Amanda's problems with reading and writing were overlooked until Amanda reached high school. An observant English teacher recommended that she be evaluated for dyslexia. "I hated to read," Amanda explains. "My mom would always pressure me to read books in my spare time, but I would make excuses. I was a slow reader, so it always took me a long time to finish something. We would argue all the time about reading.

"At school, my written work was a mess, and I've

always gotten lower grades in English because of all of the mistakes I've made with spelling, punctuation, and capitalization. Finally, this year, my English teacher said I should be tested for dyslexia."

David's symptoms were more severe. "I had so much trouble in first grade that I ended up being left back," says David. "I couldn't learn the alphabet. My teacher kept telling me to learn the letters, but I couldn't do it. I would try to remember them, but a couple of minutes later, I wouldn't have any idea what they were. My teacher was very strict, and she would lose her patience with me a lot. The worst part was having to read out loud in reading group. I would dread my turn. Since I didn't know the letters, there was no way I could know the words. Sometimes I would just sit there and not say anything, and eventually the teacher would go on to the next person. And sometimes I would make up words just to have something to say. Either way, it was really embarrassing, and the other kids would make fun of me. Finally, in third grade, I was diagnosed with dyslexia, and then things started to get better."

Many students with dyslexia have difficulty completing assignments on time because they tend to take longer to make sense out of what they are reading and to write down what they want to say. Before being diagnosed, many of these young people are criticized for being rebellious or lazy. The truth, however, is that most of them are trying their best to keep up with their classmates. Many are working even harder than other students to succeed in school, yet they often fail. Fortunately, once a diagnosis is made and once the teacher understands the nature of the disorder, these students are able to get the help they need to succeed.

"I always tried so hard to do well in school, but it didn't do any good," recalls Kristin. I was always behind everyone else. If we had to read something and then answer questions in writing, I would still be trying to read the material when everyone else was already handing in their papers. I would feel so flustered inside. Some of my teachers were patient with me, but others weren't. Many of them told me I was lazy, which infuriated me since I was working as hard as I could. After I was diagnosed with dyslexia, my teachers were a lot more understanding, which helped me to not feel so upset inside."

DIFFICULTIES WITH SCHOOLWORK

Some of the most common problems that students with dyslexia face at school include the following.

Problems with Reading

Because of their confusion over the relationship between printed words and spoken words, dyslexics tend to have trouble understanding what they are reading and have to go back over the material several times to figure out what is wrong. These students typically dread reading out loud in front of classmates because they fear being teased and ridiculed for their mistakes.

"Reading out loud in front of someone else is the worst thing I can think of," says Jennifer. "After all of the times people have made fun of my reading, I don't ever again want to be in a situation where other people can hear me read. If I need help with certain words when I'm reading to myself, I make sure to ask people I feel comfortable with, like my parents or my sister or a couple of my friends."

Problems with Spelling and Writing

Because of their confusion over how print maps to speech, dyslexic students tend to confuse, add, or omit letters in words or feel unsure of the order in which the letters should be placed in words. As a result, they typically erase, cross out, or write over their mistakes when doing

Oral presentations are difficult enough for the average student, but for a student with dyslexia, they can be unbearable. As Jennifer noted, reading aloud presents one of the most stressful situations there is.

written work. Their difficulty with spelling and their poor handwriting cause these students to turn in schoolwork and homework papers that are hard to read and often do not make sense.

"Amanda's spelling was awful," says Amanda's English teacher. "There were so many misspellings in her work that I knew she wasn't just being careless. And her papers were really a mess, with poor handwriting and many erasures. It's surprising that no one picked up on Amanda's problems a long time ago."

Problems with Math and Science

"Math has always been hard for me," says Gregory. "I sometimes switch numbers around or I get confused about whether I'm supposed to do addition or multiplication because those two signs look alike to me. My grades in math have never been good. Since I've been diagnosed with dyslexia, my math teacher tries to explain to me ahead of time what I'm supposed to do, and if I switch around any numbers, she lets me have another try at the problem. I'm doing better now."

Many students have trouble doing word problems because of the reading involved. In addition, organizing the information presented in these problems and following the sequence of steps to find the answer also tend to be difficult for dyslexics.

Sequencing problems make algebra difficult for some students. Many also have trouble following the logical steps in proof of a theorem in geometry and the order of steps involved in doing laboratory experiments in science.

Problems with History and Geography

Sequencing problems also make following dates, times, and events in history difficult for many students. Students who confuse direction often have trouble reading maps and globes in geography class. They may confuse east and west or north and south, for example.

Difficulty Taking Tests

Many dyslexic students have trouble reading test material, organizing the information, and writing down the answers. Timed tests put added pressure on these students because the nature of their condition causes them to work slowly.

"How could I do well on a test when I had so much trouble with reading and writing?" asks Lisa. "There were so many times that I would still be trying to figure out the questions when other kids were handing in their papers. I'm a shy person, and it made me feel even more self-conscious when everyone would be getting up to turn in their papers and I was still sitting there struggling. I can remember many times breaking out in a soaking sweat and feeling my heart throbbing in my head."

Ryan says, "I would never be able to get to sleep the night before a test. I would study hard and I would know the material, but I would also know that it wouldn't do any good because I wouldn't be able to finish the test anyway. I always felt angry, but I never said anything to anyone because I seemed to be the only one having a problem."

Difficulty Completing Reports and Term Papers

Reading is an essential skill when doing research. Because of their characteristic problems with reading, spelling, and writing, students with dyslexia usually have a great deal of trouble completing reports and term papers on time—or completing them at all.

"Before I was diagnosed with dyslexia, there were times that my teachers would hand back my school assignments or reports unread," says Ryan. "They were angry about my sloppy work. When I would tell them that I was doing the best that I could, they would accuse me of being defiant. My parents didn't understand that I had a problem, and if the teacher told them I was being defiant, they would go along with it and punish me."

Difficulty Copying, Taking Notes, and Understanding Lectures

When students with dyslexia try to copy something from the chalkboard in class, they often lose their place, erase frequently, misspell words, leave out capitalization and punctuation, reverse letters or words, and work very slowly.

Because of their problems with spelling, writing, and mishearing what has been said, and remembering what has been said, students with dyslexia tend to have difficulty understanding a teacher's lecture and taking notes. They may end up with only pieces of information or with incorrect information.

Problems Completing Assignments

Many students have trouble completing all of the assignments that are expected of them. Some dyslexics have trouble following their teachers' instructions, especially when the instructions involve several steps. They are likely to end up with only bits and pieces of instructions, which tend to become jumbled and confused in their minds. Also, because of their problems with reading, writing, and organizing themselves, they tend to work slowly and cannot complete their work on time.

"My work was never finished on time," says David. "Before I was diagnosed with dyslexia, I missed so many recesses because I had to stay in and finish my work instead. Even then, I sometimes couldn't finish it all. After I was diagnosed, things got a little better because my teacher gave me less work than the other kids. That way, I could finish when they did. I was happier then because I could keep up with the other kids and not have them constantly making fun of me and calling me 'stupid' and 'dud head.' I don't think they even knew that I had less work to do than they did."

Jeff recalls, "I never had any free time after school because it took me so long to do my homework. I resented that my brothers could do what they wanted after school, but I had to stay home and finish my work. I felt like a prisoner. I wanted to join the wrestling team, but my parents wouldn't let me because my grades were low. They said I had to concentrate harder on my homework so that I would get better grades. What they didn't understand was that I was trying hard. I was trying as hard as I could, and I still had trouble."

Arriving Late for School and Forgetting Things

Students who have difficulty with the concept of time passing, and trouble organizing themselves and their belongings, tend to be late for school and to forget their books and notebooks. Many even forget to take homework back to school the following day.

"Even though my brother helps me pack my backpack the night before, I still have trouble getting myself together for school in the morning," says Gregory. "I'm always late for the school bus and I always have to run. I'm lucky because the bus driver waits for me. She calls me Sprint."

Because of their problems with space and time, some students with dyslexia get lost on their way to class and arrive late.

"When I got to middle school and had to change classrooms all day, I started getting detention for being late for class," says Tim. "My teachers were always so angry with me for getting there after the bell had rung, and they always accused me of fooling around instead of trying to get to class on time. What was so frustrating for me was that I was concentrating on getting there, but I would get lost along the way. Even though I had the same classes in the same classrooms every day, I would still get lost. That's the funny thing about dyslexia. I just couldn't help it, even though I wanted to. The embarrassment of getting to class late and having everyone look at me like there was something wrong with me was enough to make me want to get it right the next time. But the next time was always the same as the last time."

Facing Criticism and Ridicule

Until students are diagnosed and receive special instruction, they usually face a great deal of criticism. Even though they are trying their best and often are working harder than their classmates, they always seem to fail. It is common for them to constantly hear, "Why don't you ever listen?" or "Your problem is that you're not trying hard enough." This constant criticism and failure often affect their self-esteem. Some even feel they want to give up on school altogether.

"School was a nightmare," says Lisa, who finally dropped out during her freshman year of high school. "I was having so much trouble in all of my subjects, and my grades were horrible. The other kids were always making fun of me. They called me 'stupid' and 'dead head.' No one wanted to hang around with me. I started cutting school and walking to the stables where I take horseback riding lessons. I always felt better when I was with the horses. I eventually dropped out of school and started spending all of my time at the stables helping out with the horses."

STRATEGIES FOR SUCCESS

Despite all of the difficulties that dyslexics face in school, there are ways for these students to cope with the challenges and succeed in school.

As discussed in Chapter Three, the most successful approach to helping dyslexics with their problems is to give them special instruction that meets their individual needs. In fact, students with dyslexia are entitled by law to receive this type of special education. It is the job of special educators, classroom teachers, and tutors to teach these students using methods that are most appropriate for and beneficial to them—particularly multisensory structured language instruction.

In addition to special instruction, teachers and students can use a number of other strategies that are also effective in compensating for the problems that dyslexic students confront.

Strategies to Improve Reading

Reading is an essential skill to all types of learning. When dyslexic students are able to read and comprehend material more effectively, they will be more successful in all their studies.

- *Read at a comfortable level.* Many students understand more of what they read when they read textbooks written on a lower reading level than the books their classmates use. The same material is often covered in these simpler books.

- *Avoid oral reading.* Because students with dyslexia usually dread reading out loud in front of other people for fear of embarrassment, the student can practice reading aloud privately with a teacher or tutor.

- *Tape reading material.* Many students find it helpful to have someone record reading material, such as textbook reading assignments, on a tape recorder for them. They can listen to the tape while following along in their books and can go back to review parts that confuse them.

  "Once my parents and sister started taping my reading material for me, doing my school assignments became easier," says Jennifer. "If I have trouble understanding something, I can listen to that part of the tape as many times as I need to. I also can finish my work faster because I don't have to struggle through trying to make sense out of what I'm reading."

• *Listen to books on tape.* Most public libraries have books on tape. The audiocassettes can be checked out alone, or the books can be checked out at the same time, so that students can listen to the tape while following along in the book. Listening to books on tape can help students to better understand the written material.

• *Watch videos or educational television.* Many interesting and informative programs are available on videotape or through educational television. Students can use these sources to gather information for reports and projects or can use them to better understand a certain subject matter. They can be used either in place of reading material or to supplement material.

Strategies to Improve Test Results

Students whose teachers make the following allowances are generally more able to improve their test performance.

• *Allow extra time.* Because students with dyslexia tend to have trouble reading, organizing information, and answering questions in a fixed amount of time, having extra time to complete the test can make a difference in their scores.

"Now that I'm allowed to take extra time on my tests, my grades are better," says Ryan. "Some of my teachers even give me untimed tests, which really helps me."

• *Read test questions aloud.* Students often benefit from their teachers reading the test questions to them or taping the test questions so that the students can look at the words of the questions while hearing them spoken. With this method, they are less likely to misunderstand the questions.

- *Give oral tests.* Students often prefer to take oral rather than written tests because they do not have to worry about writing down any information. These tests can be in the form of conversations between them and their teachers. It is also possible for students to dictate their answers to someone else, who can write down the answers for them.

"On essay tests, my teachers give me oral tests," says Amanda. "Then I don't have to worry about misspelling words or about the problems I have with capitalization, punctuation, and handwriting."

Strategies to Improve Written Work

The following strategies can help students work around problems with reading, spelling, and handwriting when doing reports and term papers.

- *Use a tape recorder or word processor.* Rather than doing research by reading books or articles on a topic, students can gather information by talking to people who are knowledgeable about the subject. Videotapes and educational television programs are also good sources of information. After the interviewing and research have been completed, the student can make an oral presentation to the teacher or to the class, or the material can be recorded on a tape recorder and presented on tape.

Sometimes writing is necessary, however. A word processor equipped with a spell-check program can be a big help. Students will not have to struggle with handwriting and spelling, and it is more likely that they will complete assignments on time because the word processor often helps them to write faster.

"Now that I'm doing my written assignments on our word processor, things have changed for the better," says Ryan. "My work is neat, and the words are

A word processor with a spell-check program can be a big help to a person with dyslexia. Without the stress of writing and spelling, a student can be free to take notes and concentrate on his or her learning.

spelled correctly. Now my teachers aren't accusing me of being defiant anymore, and my parents aren't punishing me."

STRATEGIES FOR SUCCESS IN SCHOOL:

- **HAVING READING MATERIAL TAPED**
- **BEING ALLOWED EXTRA TIME ON TESTS**
- **BEING ASSIGNED LESS HOMEWORK**
- **USING A TAPE RECORDER OR WORD PROCESSOR FOR REPORTS AND TERM PAPERS**
- **HAVING HELP WITH INSTRUCTIONS**

Amanda says, "I'm doing so much better in English now that I use a word processor for my written assignments. I don't have to worry about poor handwriting or misspelled words. I'm getting better grades, which makes me feel good."

- *Avoid lectures and note taking.* Because many students have trouble understanding and remembering lectures and taking notes, teachers can help by using other teaching methods. When lecture instruction is necessary, however, students can ask someone else to take notes for them, or they can record the lecture on tape so that they can listen to it as many times as necessary in order to understand and remember the material.

- *Have extra time and less work to complete.* To compensate for their tendency to work slowly, most students welcome being allowed extra time to complete assignments or being given less work to complete. Teachers might assign every other problem, rather than every problem, on a math page or require students to write only half a page, rather than two full pages, for a report. This approach will help most students feel less frustrated, and as a result they will more likely produce better work.

- *Have adjusted homework assignments.* Dyslexic students are grateful and relieved when teachers assign them less homework or allow them to use word processors and tape recorders for written assignments. This way, they have free time for afterschool activities or to develop other important skills.

"Now that I've been diagnosed with dyslexia, my teachers give me less homework," says Jeff. "I finally have time to do what I want to do after school. I don't have to feel like a prisoner anymore. I still have to work hard on my schoolwork, but at least I have some free time after school now. And my parents are a lot more understanding. They even let me join the wrestling team, and I'm undefeated this year."

Strategies to Improve In-Class Achievement

Teachers can use some of these strategies to ensure students' success in the classroom.

- *Make lists.* Lists can help students keep track of what they need to do. Teachers can write the steps of classroom assignments on an index card, in a notebook, or on self-stick notepaper—whatever works best for the student.

- *Seat the students at the front of the classroom.* Sitting closer to the chalkboard can help students to concentrate better. Those who sit at the front of the classroom can also benefit from being given different work by the teacher without their classmates knowing and from getting help from the teacher when necessary.

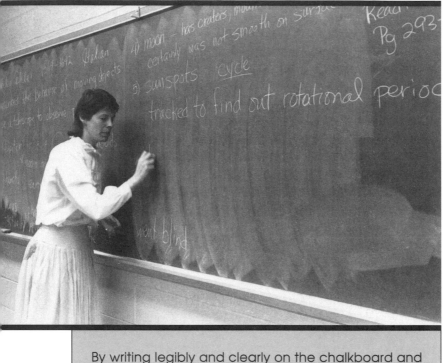

By writing legibly and clearly on the chalkboard and speaking directly to the class, a teacher can help a student with dyslexia. These actions help to maintain a structured, organized learning environment.

• *Provide structure and clarity.* Most students with dyslexia seem to do best in a well-organized, predictable classroom environment. Teachers can help by keeping books and supplies in the same place every day and by keeping instructions simple and consistent.

Students appreciate teachers who write clearly and legibly on the chalkboard and when making corrections on their papers. They also do better when teachers speak clearly and slowly during class.

- *Offer praise and understanding.* Praise from teachers helps encourage students to try again after making mistakes and to believe that they can be successful at learning.

Students with dyslexia also benefit when they feel that teachers understand that they are working hard, that they need extra attention, and that being dyslexic is very frustrating for them.

GOING ON TO COLLEGE

Many young people with dyslexia have successfully completed a college degree program. To achieve this goal, however, students must be willing to work hard. In addition, to ensure students' success, some special provisions can be made by the college—such as providing tutoring, allowing students to use a computer or word processor for written assignments, allowing students extra time on tests or giving them oral tests, and allowing them to tape record lectures.

Special accommodations are available to eligible students who are taking certain college entrance examinations. For example, both the Scholastic Assessment Test (SAT) and the American College Testing (ACT) Assessment are available in large-type format and on audiocassette. Additionally, students may elect to take these tests on an extended-time basis, whereby they are allowed a certain amount of extra testing time. School guidance counselors can provide information about college admissions tests for students with special needs. They also can provide information about colleges with programs designed for dyslexic students. These colleges have set up special programs that emphasize small class size and individual attention.

Chapter Five

GETTING ALONG WITH FAMILY AND FRIENDS

Dyslexia affects not only the individuals who have the condition, but also their parents, siblings, classmates, and teammates. Young people with dyslexia often have a tough time growing up. They tend to be misunderstood by others. Many work hard in school and want to succeed, but their school performance does not reflect their effort. They are likely to be criticized or punished by parents and teachers for not trying hard enough, and teased by classmates and friends for being stupid, sloppy, or strange. Making and keeping friends are often very difficult, also. As a result, friction tends to develop between them and the other people in their lives. Many end up feeling frustrated and inadequate. They may resort to defiant behavior or become shy and withdrawn.

For those young people with dyslexia who reach adolescence without being diagnosed or helped, the hardships they face are likely to be worse both academically and emotionally because of the many years of failure and criticism that they have endured. Some give up trying to do well at school, adopting a "Why bother?" attitude. Others become loners and avoid participating in social activities so that they do not have to face ridicule from their peers. Still others feel resentful of the constant criticism and rejection and resort to angry or defiant behavior, as Tim and Jennifer did.

Some teenagers with dyslexia develop psychosomatic ailments, such as headaches or stomachaches, as a result of the stress and anxiety they feel from constant criticism by others. Lisa developed headaches. "I used to get a sharp pain across my forehead," says Lisa. "The pain would get worse as the school day went on because my teachers would pick apart my work and tell me that I wasn't applying myself. My mom took me to one doctor after another, but they never found anything wrong. The pain stopped after I quit school."

In most cases, once a diagnosis is made, the situation improves. The person with dyslexia is relieved to find there is an explanation for the problems and feels hopeful upon hearing about the ways he or she can be helped. Family members, teachers, and classmates usually become more understanding and patient, too.

Lisa is back in school now and is working a day at a time to get back on track. "Now that I've been diagnosed with dyslexia, my parents and teachers are trying to make learning easier for me," she says. They're careful to not criticize me and to work with me on completing my assignments. I'm beginning to feel that I may be able to do some things right after all."

RELATIONSHIPS WITH PARENTS

Like all young people, those with dyslexia want their parents to feel proud of them. Unfortunately, because of the nature of the disorder, their efforts to succeed often end in failure, and criticism and punishment from parents often become commonplace. As a result, some of these young people develop defiant behavior toward their parents, while others become so discouraged that they totally give up trying to succeed.

YOUNG PEOPLE WITH DYSLEXIA ARE OFTEN MISUNDERSTOOD BY FAMILY MEMBERS, TEACHERS, CLASSMATES, AND TEAMMATES.

"There was no pleasing my parents," recalls Ryan. "They put a lot of emphasis on school and grades, but school was so hard for me that I never did well. They expected me to bring home A's and B's and instead I brought home mostly C's and D's, and sometimes even F's. Except in art, I don't remember ever getting a grade higher than a C before I was diagnosed with dyslexia. Regardless of how hard I tried, I just couldn't measure up to my parents' expectations. They constantly criticized me for being lazy and for being a disappointment to them. I felt sad that they were disappointed in me, but I also felt angry about them always punishing me for my bad grades.

"I used to spend a lot of time in my room with my door locked. I would just sit and draw and block out my parents and my problems. My parents weren't very happy about my drawing, either. They said it was a waste of the time I could have spent on my schoolwork. What they didn't understand was that, without help for my problems, there was no way I could have done any better in school than I was doing."

Ryan's mother says, "My husband and I were good students. We went to school together, and our grades were quite good. It really hurt us to know that our son was such a poor student. We just expected that he would do as well in school as we had. It was difficult for us to accept his failures, and we ended up arguing with him all the time. And eventually, my husband and I began arguing with each other. Our home life was so stressful and unpleasant."

Typically, once a diagnosis is made and parents understand dyslexia, they come to realize that the problems their sons and daughters have had could not have been helped. Most realize the need to be patient and understanding.

"Since my diagnosis, I've been getting along a lot better with my parents," Ryan says. "They do what they can to help me with my work, and they're not so hung up on my grades anymore. And they've stopped nagging me about the time I spend on my artwork. They even encourage me to enter contests and exhibits now."

Ryan's father says, "Once we understood about dyslexia, my wife and I realized that Ryan was doing his best and that we had to support his efforts. He's making slow progress at school, and his grades have improved slightly. All we can ask of him is that he try as hard as possible. And I must admit, he is a gifted artist. Neither my wife nor I has any talent in art, and we're constantly amazed at the beautiful work he produces."

RELATIONSHIPS WITH BROTHERS AND SISTERS

Before a diagnosis is made, young people with dyslexia are likely to feel inadequate or envious in their relationships with their brothers and sisters who are not dyslexic. The struggle that dyslexics have with schoolwork and the poor grades they so often receive tend to make these young people feel inferior to sisters and brothers who do well in school and envious of the praise their siblings receive for success. The relationship among siblings is made worse when the dyslexic brother or sister is teased or ridiculed for his or her weaknesses.

"My brothers always seemed to be so perfect," says Jeff. "I'm the youngest in our family, and I had to go all through school behind the two of them. They got great grades and did well in sports. One of my brothers also plays the saxophone really well. I just couldn't measure up. When my parents wouldn't let me join the wrestling team because I was doing so poorly in school, it was really hard for me to accept that my brothers were allowed to play sports and I wasn't. They even teased me about it sometimes, which really made me mad."

Siblings sometimes grow to resent or envy a dyslexic brother or sister because he or she receives extra attention from the parents when trying to complete homework assignments, studying for tests, and finishing chores around the house. The extra time that parents spend with a dyslexic son or daughter sometimes causes other children in the family to feel neglected. The result is often fighting among the siblings, which adds to the tension at home.

"My mom has always had to spend a lot of time with Kristin on her schoolwork, and I used to resent that she spent so much extra time with her," says Kristin's sister, Megan. "I used to pick fights with Kristin because, even though I knew it was wrong, I wanted to get back at her for taking my mom's time away from me. My mom was really upset about our fighting, and she took us to talk to a counselor, who helped me to realize that I might feel better if I helped my sister with her schoolwork. That's the way we've been working things out, and I really feel a lot better about everything. I feel important now."

RELATIONSHIPS WITH PEERS

When young people with dyslexia stumble over words when reading or speaking, they are likely to be laughed at by their classmates and called "stupid." When their handwriting is poor, they are likely to be picked on for being "sloppy." When they go off on a topic different from what everyone else is talking about, they are likely to be called "strange."

"I can remember one time in second grade when I read out loud in reading group and messed up on most of the words," recalls David. "I was so embarrassed that I almost

ONCE DIAGNOSED, YOUNG PEOPLE WITH DYSLEXIA ARE USUALLY RELIEVED TO UNDERSTAND THE CAUSE OF THEIR PROBLEMS, AND FEEL HOPEFUL TO LEARN THAT THERE ARE WAYS TO OVERCOME THEM.

hyperventilated. The teacher ended up calling on someone else to read it correctly, which only embarrassed me more. That day at recess, my best friend told me that he didn't want to be friends with me anymore because I was too stupid. I cried myself to sleep that night over it, but in a way, I didn't really blame him because I wouldn't have wanted to be friends with somebody like me either."

The problems that young people with dyslexia face in school also create problems for them outside of school. They may be shunned by classmates after school, for example, or ridiculed by teammates during sports activities, as Tim was.

RESOLVING CONFLICT

Friction between young people with dyslexia and other people in their lives usually begins to subside after everyone gains a better understanding of the condition. Parents tend to ease up on their demands and expectations, and most siblings want to help their dyslexic brother or sister. Even classmates and teammates tend to show compassion once they learn about dyslexia.

"After I was diagnosed with dyslexia and started getting help at school and at home, things changed for the better," says David. "Since I had gotten left back in first grade and since so many kids called me names like 'stupid' and 'dud head,' I thought I was stupid. But after I had help for awhile, I started to feel that maybe I wasn't stupid after all. The best part was that the other kids stopped teasing me, and they wanted to hang around me more."

Here are some of the ways in which family members and friends can help young people with dyslexia cope with the disorder and achieve success:

- *Encourage reading.* By keeping interesting reading materials around the house, parents can make reading more inviting. Many young people also feel more like reading when family members sit in the same room and also read. Some enjoy having a family member read to them.

- *Help with homework.* Having a parent or a brother or sister stay nearby to give help or to check completed homework assignments can be beneficial to students with dyslexia. Keeping the house quiet and free of distractions can also help.

- *Tape textbook material.* When family members or friends record textbook material on a tape recorder, the dyslexic student can listen to the tape while following along in the textbook. This simple technique often makes it easier for him or her to understand the written material.

- *Keep instructions simple.* Parents can help by keeping instructions for household chores short and simple and by giving only one instruction at a time whenever possible. When longer or more complex instructions are necessary, parents can help by writing instructions on an index card.

- *Help discover and develop a talent or hobby.* Parents can help their son or daughter discover and develop a talent or hobby. Becoming good at an activity or knowing a lot about a subject can balance the frustration and pain that dyslexics feel from being teased and criticized.

Discovering a hobby, skill, or a special talent is one way to develop confidence and self-esteem. Becoming good at something can balance the frustration that a dyslexic teen often feels after experiencing difficulty in other areas.

- *Keep the home routine regular.* Young people with dyslexia function best when the home routine is kept regular. Parents can help by sticking to a set dinnertime and bedtime, for example.

- *Show support and give praise.* Young people with dyslexia need family and friends who will accept them, regardless of their problems. They are able to feel better about themselves when family and friends support their efforts by attending games or performances, for example, and praise them for their accomplishments.

Jeff says, "My brothers don't tease me anymore. They come to all of my wrestling matches, which lets me know that they care about me, and that really makes me feel good."

• *Be good listeners.* By listening to what young people with dyslexia have to say, family members and friends are showing that they are interested in their opinions and are concerned about their feelings. Also by listening, family members and friends will be better able to understand what these young people are going through and where they need particular help.

In the next chapter, the young people in this book tell how they are successfully coping with dyslexia in their everyday lives, and they share their dreams for the future.

Chapter Six

THE POWER OF SELF-ESTEEM

The development of self-esteem, or how we feel about ourselves and our abilities, is a process that begins early in life. Throughout our childhood, the way in which we are treated by others shapes how we feel about ourselves. Children who have been praised by people around them tend to feel good about themselves and can develop a positive self-image. Children who have been criticized and punished by people around them tend not to feel good about themselves and are likely to develop a negative self-image. In order to mature into well-adjusted adults, it is important that children learn to feel good about themselves.

THE EFFECTS OF DYSLEXIA ON SELF-ESTEEM

Young people with dyslexia often suffer from low self-esteem as a result of the ridicule and rejection they receive from other people. Years of criticism and punishment from parents and teachers and teasing from classmates and friends leave many of them feeling inferior or worthless. They feel bad that they have not lived up to the expectations of their parents and teachers and that they are not accepted by their peers.

Ryan says, "I knew I was a disappointment to my parents because they would always say, 'Where did we go wrong?' and 'Why can't you do well in school?' What they didn't understand was that I couldn't help the way I was. I was trying hard, but it didn't do any good. I felt awful about letting them down, though. I hated myself, and I would have given anything to have been a different person."

Constant failure also contributed to Lisa's low self-esteem. "I always felt like a misfit. My grades at school were the worst. I was failing almost every subject. I hated school and didn't see the use in trying anymore because, even though I would try hard, I would still fail. When I started cutting classes, my parents kept grounding me, and I got some suspensions from school. I knew I was doing wrong, but I didn't care because I didn't do anything right anyway. I felt worthless."

> **Y**OUNG PEOPLE WITH DYSLEXIA OFTEN SUFFER FROM LOW SELF-ESTEEM AS A RESULT OF THE RIDICULE AND REJECTION THEY RECEIVE FROM OTHER PEOPLE.

As you know, people with dyslexia experience the symptoms of the condition in different ways and at different levels of severity. The level of severity of the symptoms they experience tends to affect how they feel about themselves. For example, those who have mild symptoms may find that being dyslexic is more of a nuisance than a disability.

Amanda says, "I knew I had trouble with spelling and writing, and I knew I was a slow reader, but these things were never that big of a deal to me because my grades were okay, except in English. And I've always had a lot of friends."

Dyslexics who have moderate symptoms confront much more failure and criticism. As a result, they are likely to find it difficult to feel good about themselves.

Jeff says, "Until I became undefeated in wrestling, I felt inferior to my brothers in every way because they always did everything well, especially in school. They've always been on the honor roll."

People with severe symptoms usually face the greatest amount of ridicule and rejection from others. They usually live with constant criticism and a constant sense of failure. As a result, it is common for them to have low self-esteem.

DEVELOPING A POSITIVE SELF-IMAGE

All of us, whether we are dyslexic or not, feel better about ourselves every time we successfully reach a goal. Think about the first time you scored a run while playing baseball, for instance, or the first time you were able to sing a song from beginning to end. You probably felt proud of your accomplishment and good about yourself, which raised your self-esteem.

Here are some strategies that young people with dyslexia can use to build a more positive self-image:

- *Set reasonable goals.* Goals that are reasonable tend to be attainable, whereas goals that are too difficult tend not to be attainable. By setting reasonable goals, young people are likely to attain them and can feel proud of their accomplishment each time they do so.

- *Focus on strengths.* Many young people have found that focusing on activities they do well can earn them praise, which in turn helps them to develop self-confidence in other areas. Kristin excels in dancing ballet and has been chosen to dance in many performances. Ryan entered his artwork in a statewide art contest and won first prize, and Lisa won second place in a horseback riding show.

Schools and community groups often offer classes in art, music, or dance, or organized team sports, such as football, baseball, basketball, and soccer. Many also offer individual sports, such as tennis, wrestling, gymnastics, and swimming.

Jeff says, "I may not be able to make the honor roll, but at least I've achieved being the only wrestler in our school who's undefeated. I feel proud of that, and my family is proud of me, too."

All young people, both those with dyslexia and those without, thrive on encouragement and support. Family members and friends can show their enthusiasm by attending games, performances, concerts, or exhibits in which these young people participate. "My mom and sister have never missed a show or performance I've danced in," says Kristin. "I always feel so good knowing they're out there in the audience. It makes me feel important and special."

• *Become an expert.* Knowing a lot about a certain subject or knowing how to do something well is a good way to build self-confidence. Many young people with dyslexia have practiced their skills and have become experts in a particular activity.

"I had an interest in cooking," says Amanda. "I love gourmet food, and I was always interested in knowing how those special dishes were prepared. My grandmother is a great cook, and she helped me learn some of the basics of cooking. I started with some simple recipes, like meat loaf and baked macaroni and cheese, but now I'm into more complicated dishes. My family likes it when I cook. I also do the cooking when we have company, and I get a lot of compliments."

Tim's brother, Paul, says, "Tim's model airplanes

Sports such as wrestling are a good way to build self-confidence. Belonging to a team or other organization can help a dyslexic teen reach out to others, develop talents, and explore new ideas.

are awesome. Whenever we go out to the field to fly them with our uncle, Tim gets a lot of compliments, and sometimes they're from guys who have been building planes a lot longer than Tim has."

"I feel proud when I get compliments on my airplanes," says Tim. "Building planes is the one thing I've been able to do really well. All through my life, people always seemed to notice the things I did wrong, especially in school. It feels great to finally have people notice me for something good."

• *Join clubs and organizations.* Most schools offer students opportunities to become involved in clubs, such as a computer club, chess club, drama club, or photography club. Community organizations, such as scouts, and religious youth groups also offer young people opportunities to become involved in a variety of activities. Joining clubs and organizations is a good way to gain new experiences, develop talents and skills, and make friends.

• *Get a job.* Many teenagers with dyslexia have found that working at a part-time job has helped them gain a sense of accomplishment. Knowing that they were accepted for the job and successfully meeting the responsibilities associated with it have helped them to feel proud.

Tim works a few hours each weekend in a hobby shop, where he earns money to buy the materials for his model airplanes. Lisa is still helping out at the stables and is now being paid for her time. "I love being around the horses," she says, "and the pay I get makes the situation even better because I'm saving up to buy my own horse."

• *Do volunteer work.* Sme young people with dyslexia have found volunteer work gratifying and have been able to feel good about devoting their time and effort to helping other people. Knowing that people count on them and knowing that their efforts are appreciated have helped these young people to feel good about themselves.

"During the summer, my sister and I both do volunteer work at the hospital where my dad works," says Jennifer. "We especially like helping the children. They always seem to be really happy to see us. We play games with them and give them rides up and down the hall in a wheelchair. We have as much fun as they do, I think!"

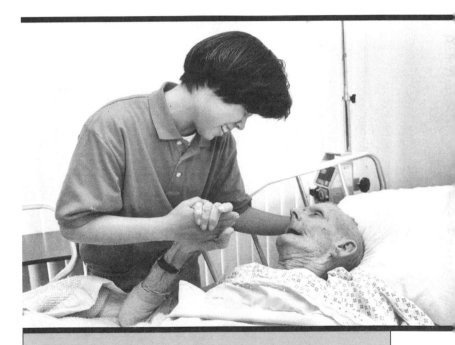

Making others feel good is one of the best ways to feel good about yourself. The benefits of volunteer work are innumerable, and for a teenager with dyslexia, they can go a very long way toward erasing doubt and insecurity.

• *Have a sense of humor.* Approaching life with a sense of humor has helped many young people cope with the hardships of being dyslexic. They have discovered that laughing at themselves when they make mistakes or making jokes out of criticisms and teasings have made these incidents less painful. Many of them have learned that having a sense of humor has also enabled them to experience happier relationships with others.

"I learned a long time ago to make a joke out of my problems," says Gregory. "I found that the other kids loved it when I would joke around. They would laugh and egg me on. I liked having all the attention focused on me.

"I still joke around about my problems, and I still like getting attention. A lot of my friends have told me that they like hanging out with me because I'm fun to be around. I may not be the best student, but I think I'm successful anyway. I have a lot of friends, and I'm happy."

• *Expect and accept setbacks.* Most young people with dyslexia know that the road to success can be bumpy and that achieving goals often takes time. Many have learned that there even will be times when trying to achieve a goal ends in failure, despite much determination and hard work. Those who can take setbacks in stride without becoming discouraged are likely to be the ones who develop a strong self-image and who will be willing to take on new challenges. They also are the ones who will be most likely to mature into well-adjusted adults.

SUCCESS STORIES

The young people you met in this book were open enough to share their stories with you—stories about the challenges presented by dyslexia and about their successes in overcoming them. Now they will share with you the stories of their lives today and their dreams for the future.

Tim

Tim is looking forward to graduating from high school and attending college. "I know that if we hadn't discovered that I was dyslexic, I never would have been able to earn good grades," he says. "The help I've gotten at school and at home has really made a difference. Now that I've been accepted to college, I'm looking forward to learning more about aeronautics. I feel that my dream of working in design engineering will finally become a reality."

"I admire Tim for his determination," says Tim's brother, Paul. "We saw how hard he had to work to earn good grades. I don't think I could have stuck with it. I know Tim will be able to finish college, and I know he'll make a great engineer."

David

David's problems were severe enough that they were recognized by the time he reached third grade, and the special instruction David received at school helped him overcome many of his problems. He attends a vocational-technical high school, where he is learning marine mechanics and is doing well.

"I wish I didn't have dyslexia, but I try not to let it get me down," David says. "I try to focus on the things I'm good at, like fixing motors and engines. I'm also a good fisherman. I do a lot of fishing near where I live, and every summer my dad and I spend a week fishing in Canada. When I'm fishing, I don't have to worry about my problems. It's the same thing with fixing motors—I don't have to worry about whether I'm good at reading or writing. After I graduate from high school next year, I'll be a mechanic at a marina."

David's father looks back on his own school experience and wonders whether his hardships were a result of dyslexia. "I struggled through school and thought I was stupid," he says. "No one ever told me otherwise. My parents didn't care much about education and never helped me with my homework. I was failing every subject. I ended up quitting school and going to work at an auto repair place changing tires. The owner took a liking to me and trained me to be a mechanic. I'm still an auto mechanic, and I enjoy my work, so I guess everything turned out okay for me.

"David seems to be doing okay, too, and I'm happy for him. He got help right at the beginning, and I think that's what made the difference between my schooling and his. I'm proud that he's going to finish school."

Gregory
Gregory approaches life with a sense of humor. "I don't let my problems ruin my life," he says. "I know I'm trying my best in school, and that's what's important to me. I'm not the best student, but that's me."

Gregory wants to become an actor and has won lead parts in school and community performances. He plans to attend a summer theater camp devoted to developing the talents of aspiring young actors. "I feel good about getting lead parts in plays," he says, "and I feel especially good after a performance when people from the audience come backstage to compliment me."

"I see myself in Gregory," says Gregory's father. "I was never a good student, but I had an outgoing personality, and I found that I could be successful by using it. I'm in sales, so I was fortunate to fall into a career that utilizes my strengths and plays down my weaknesses. I'm happy to see that Gregory has developed an outgoing personality, and I'm hoping that he'll be able to use it to find the same success and happiness in life that I have."

Lisa
Lisa went back to school and is now in tenth grade. She receives individualized instruction during the school day and also regularly meets with a tutor after school.

"We're taking things a day at a time," says Lisa's mother. "Our family has been through a lot with Lisa dropping out of school and all, but we're hopeful that we can make things work out. We didn't understand the nature of Lisa's problems and, unfortunately, we didn't handle the situation correctly. Lisa is a sensitive young lady who has many fine qualities."

Lisa says, "Now that I'm getting help with my schoolwork, things are a lot better for me. My teachers make allowances for me, and my parents don't criticize me anymore. My teachers and parents make lists and instruction cards, which have helped me to do what I'm supposed to do. At school, each of my teachers makes a list on a piece of sticky paper and gives it to me when I arrive for class. I just stick it to the top of my desk, and then I can look at it as many times as I need to. At home, we keep lists and instruction cards for what I need to do on the refrigerator and on the mirror in my room.

"I feel better about myself now that I'm starting to do things right. Things always seemed so hopeless before, but now I feel more optimistic. I'm starting to feel happy. I never thought I'd say that."

Lisa continues to work at the stables and is getting closer to her goal of being able to buy her own horse. Her grandparents have offered to pay the boarding costs. "I love working with horses," Lisa says. "Who knows, maybe I'll have my own stables someday."

Kristin

Kristin is in her senior year of high school and intends to become a professional ballerina. "Being dyslexic has forced me to work harder than most kids," she says, "but the hard work has made me a stronger person, I think. Dancing ballet requires a lot of self-discipline, and I think I'm a good dancer because I have this. And I think being a good dancer has helped me cope with my dyslexia because my accomplishments in ballet have helped me to feel good about myself. Having self-confidence has helped me get through the times when my teachers and classmates have looked down on me because of my problems at school."

Kristin has the added fortune of having a caring, supportive mother. "My mom has been a big help to me," she says. "Once we found out that I'm dyslexic, she talked to my teachers and read a lot of books to try to find out how to help me. She stays right with me when I do my homework so that if I have questions or if I get stuck on something, she can help me. She also reads all of my textbook and other reading material out loud to me, or she records it on a tape recorder. And my mom encourages me. She tells me that I'm smart and that I can succeed. She really makes me believe it."

Kristin's mother says, "Despite her problems, Kristin is a strong individual with great determination. I want her to know that she's smart and that she can achieve success in whatever she chooses to do with her life. Being dyslexic might put a few hurdles along her path, but I know she'll do fine."

Jennifer
With the help of her parents and sister, Jennifer continues to make progress in school. In addition to receiving individualized instruction at school to help correct her problems, Jennifer also is allowed to use a word processor for her written work and is given extra time to complete assignments and tests. At home, Jennifer's parents and sister continue to help Jennifer with her reading assignments. Although she still sometimes mispronounces words and mishears what is being said, she is learning to take these problems in stride.

"I don't get so upset over my mistakes anymore," Jennifer says. "I used to blame everyone else for why I misheard what was said, but now I understand that, for me, mishearing is part of being dyslexic. It's nobody's fault. My parents and sister are doing everything they can to help me, and I appreciate that. We don't argue anymore, and I'm glad."

STRATEGIES FOR DEVELOPING A POSITIVE SELF-IMAGE

- **SETTING REASONABLE GOALS**
- **FOCUSING ON STRENGTHS**
- **JOINING CLUBS AND ORGANIZATIONS**
- **DOING VOLUNTEER WORK**
- **HAVING A SENSE OF HUMOR**

Jennifer is one of the top divers on the girls' swim team at her school. "I feel so free when I'm diving," she says. "When I'm at practice or in a competition, no one cares whether I mispronounce words or mishear what other people are saying. Excelling at diving has helped me feel good about myself because I get a lot of praise and because the kids at school seem to know me for my diving and not for the problems I have with my schoolwork."

Jennifer hopes to attend college and medical school. "The volunteer work my sister and I do during the summer has inspired me to become a doctor," she says. "I know it will be a lot of really hard work, and maybe it's a long shot for me, but I'm willing to try. I want to help kids who have cancer."

Amanda

Amanda is making progress in her first year of high school. She regularly meets with a tutor, who gives her enough extra help with her schoolwork to ensure that she earns good grades. Amanda's teachers also have helped by making certain allowances for her. By letting her do her written assignments on a word processor, for example, they have enabled Amanda to work around her problems with spelling and handwriting. Additionally, on essay tests, her teachers give her oral tests rather than written ones.

Amanda wore braces a few years ago and admires the work of her orthodontist. "I want to be an orthodontist someday," she says. "I'll have to get through college and dental school, though. I know I'll have to work harder than most kids because of my dyslexia, but I'm not afraid to work hard. I'm doing well in school right now, so my hard work is already paying off."

Ryan
"Things are much better now that I've been diagnosed with dyslexia," says Ryan. "Now that there's an explanation for why school has always been so hard for me, my parents don't pick on me anymore. And they finally give me credit for trying my best."

Ryan wants to be a graphic artist. "Winning first place in the art contest in our state really meant a lot to me," he says. "It's the first thing I've ever done that I've been able to feel proud of."

Jeff
Jeff feels that the special instruction he receives and the allowances his teachers have made have helped him improve his school performance.

"With the help I'm getting, doing my schoolwork is easier for me, and I'm doing better," he says. "I work really hard for my grades, though. Being diagnosed with dyslexia explained why I could never measure up to my brothers, and now that we know that I have a problem and they don't, the pressure is off of me to compete with them. All that matters now is that I do the best I can, and it's okay if my achievements aren't the same as theirs.

"My parents say they're proud of me for doing my best in school. They also say they're proud of my undefeated record in wrestling, and they make a point of coming to all of my matches. I think I wrestle better knowing they're out there supporting me."

Jeff wants to join the Navy after he graduates from high school. "Getting into the Navy is really important to me, and I know I can't mess up in school. I keep that in mind when I'm doing my schoolwork."

RESOURCES

Learning Disabilities Association of America
4156 Library Road
Pittsburgh, PA 15234

LDA is a nonprofit organization with 50 state affiliates and more than 600 local chapters. LDA is concerned with finding and exploring solutions for many types of learning problems, including those that result from dyslexia.

National Center for Learning Disabilities
381 Park Avenue South, Suite 1420
New York, NY 10016

NCLD is a national nonprofit organization dedicated to improving the lives of people affected by learning disabilities. It strives to raise public awareness and understanding of children and adults with learning disabilities and to provide national leadership on their behalf.

National Information Center for Children
and Youth with Disabilities
P.O. Box 1492
Washington, D.C. 20013-1492

NICHCY is an information clearinghouse that provides
information on disabilities and disability-related issues.
Children and youth (from birth to age twenty-two) are the
focus of its attention. NICHCY's services include answering questions about disability issues, assisting parents and
professional groups on technical matters, providing publications, providing information from its databases and
libraries, and making referrals to other organizations.

Orton Dyslexia Society
Chester Building, Suite 382
8600 LaSalle Road
Baltimore, MD 21286

The Orton Dyslexia Society is a nonprofit organization
founded in 1949. It was established to continue the efforts
of Samuel T. Orton, a doctor who was a pioneer in the
study and treatment of dyslexia. The Orton Dyslexia Society has more than forty branches across the United States,
as well as branches in Canada and Israel. Each branch
office provides information, sponsors conferences, and
refers people to groups that offer other services.

GLOSSARY

consonant: any letter of the alphabet that is not a vowel and that is a speech sound produced by stopping or slowing the passage of air

diagnosis: the process of identifying a disorder, such as dyslexia, on the basis of particular symptoms, characteristics, and test patterns

dyslexia: a language communication disability

dyslexic: a person who has the condition dyslexia

grade level: a standard for achievement comparable to the equivalent grade in school

intelligence: the ability to learn or understand or to deal with new situations

language: a system of communication by means of spoken or written symbols

multisensory structured language instruction: a type of instruction that benefits dyslexic learners; it is individualized, multisensory, systematic, and sequential, and involves direct instruction in phonics

peers: a group of individuals belonging to the same group in society by age, grade, or status; for example, friends, classmates, or teammates

phoneme: the smallest sound unit in a language

phonics: a method of teaching beginners to read and pronounce words by learning the speech sounds related to letters and groups of letters

phonological awareness: the ability to appreciate that spoken language is made up of individually distinct sound units

psychologist: a professional who helps people with problems of behavior

reading: a linguistic process of decoding and giving meaning to speech that has been written down in symbols

reading level: the level at which a child is reading, usually expressed in terms of grade level

remediation: the process of correcting problems, such as those associated with dyslexia

reversals: changing the position or orientation of letters, numbers, parts of words, or whole words

self-image: how a person sees himself or herself and how this individual perceives that others see him or her

sequencing: placing ideas, events, letters, and words in logical or chronological order, and numbers in a certain numerical order

sibling: a brother or sister

standardized test: a test with specific procedures and certain tasks, and for which norms have been established so that comparable measurements may be obtained in different geographical regions

syllable: part of a word pronounced as a unit that usually consists of a vowel alone or a vowel with one or more consonants

symptom: a sign, mark, or signal that points to the existence of something else

tutor: a person who gives instruction and guidance to another, usually on a one-to-one basis

vowel: the letters "a," "e," "i," "o," "u," and sometimes "y," which are speech sounds produced by the air passage not being blocked or constricted

FURTHER READING

For Children and Teenagers

Cummings, Rhoda, and Gary Fisher. *The Survival Guide for Teenagers with LD* (*Learning Differences)*. Minneapolis: Free Spirit Publishing Inc., 1993.

Fisher, Gary, and Rhoda Cummings. *The Survival Guide for Kids with LD* (*Learning Differences)*. Minneapolis: Free Spirit Publishing Inc., 1990.

Gehret, Jeanne. *The Don't-Give-Up Kid and Learning Disabilities*. Fairport, NY: Verbal Images Press, 1990.

Hall, David E. *Living with Learning Disabilities: A Guide for Students*. Minneapolis: Lerner Publications Company, 1993.

Janover, Caroline. *Joshua: A Boy with Dyslexia*. Burlington, VT: Waterfront Books, 1988.

Knox, Jean McBee. *Learning Disabilities*. New York: Chelsea House, 1989.

Landau, Elaine. *Dyslexia*. New York: Franklin Watts, 1991.

Lewis, Marjorie. *Wrongway Applebaum*. New York: Coward-McCann, 1984.

Savage, John. *Dyslexia: Understanding Reading Problems.* New York: Julian Messner, 1985.

For Parents, Teachers, and Older Readers

Coles, Gerald. *The Learning Mystique: A Critical Look at "Learning Disabilities."* New York: Pantheon Books, 1988.

Hornsby, Beve. *Overcoming Dyslexia: A Straightforward Guide for Families and Teachers.* London: Macdonald Optima, 1988.

Huston, Anne Marshall. *Understanding Dyslexia: A Practical Approach for Parents and Teachers.* Lanham, MD: Madison Books, 1992.

MacCracken, Mary. *Turnabout Children.* Boston: Little, Brown & Co., 1986.

Roswell, Florence G., and Gladys Natchez. *Reading Disability: A Human Approach to Evaluation and Treatment of Reading and Writing Difficulties.* New York: Basic Books, 1989.

INDEX